The Wild Life of LOVE

The Wild Life of LOVE

A RUBES® CARTOON COLLECTION

BY LEIGH RUBIN

WILLOW CREEK PRESS

For Teresa — You drive me wild!

The individual cartoons in this collection have been previously published in newspaper syndication.
RUBES® is syndicated internationally by Creators Syndicate, Inc. and licensed by Leigh Rubin.

Published by Willow Creek Press
P.O. Box 147, Minocqua, Wisconsin 54548

Library of Congress Cataloging-in-Publication Data: On file

Printed in Canada

According to the popular song, "Birds do it, bees do it" and "even educated fleas do it." But what about snails and whales? Or tortoises and porpoises? Or for that matter, how about sharks, spiders, penguins, and porcupines? (Ouch!) I would imagine they are all doing it too. But did you ever wonder if all these creatures experience the same joy, jealousy, passion, pain, frustration and happiness that love brings? And speaking of animals, what about us? Doesn't love bring out our "wild" side? Maybe we're more alike than we think. After all, according to another popular song,"love is all we need."

WHY, DARLING, OF COURSE YOU'RE THE ONLY ONE FOR ME, PROVIDING OF COURSE THAT YOU'RE THE ONE I THINK YOU ARE.
Leigh

LOVER'S LEAP
ON THE COUNT OF THREE... ONE, TWO, THREE...
LOVER'S LEAP
WELL, AT LEAST WE TRIED.

...THEY SLIPPED BEHIND THE BARN AND QUICKLY REMOVED EACH OTHER'S HARNESS. THERE, WITH NOTHING TO REIN THEM IN, IT WOULD BE A NIGHT OF UNBRIDLED PASSION.
TRUE HORSE ROMANCE

Virgin wool.

Contrary to popular belief, not all dinosaurs were cold-blooded.

ISN'T THAT ROMANTIC? THEY WERE ONLY HERE A WEEK AGO AND THEY'RE ALREADY RENEWING THEIR VOWS!
LOVER'S LEAP
Leigh

"Hey, sorry, pal. But you know what they say, 'Love hurts.'"

"Ah, young love! Why, I remember my first kiss—all wet and slimy... Just like out of a fairy tale!"

One can only imagine the extent of Vinnie's embarrassment after waking up hung over next to a lawn ornament.

"It pains me to tell you this, Herb, but I'm afraid I can't see you anymore."

One rhino's desperate attempt to save the species.

"Well, son, there's really not much to explain about the birds and the bees... You see, your mother and I got you from a seed catalog."

WHY DON'T YOU RELAX WHILE I GO UPSTAIRS AND METAMORPHOSE INTO SOMETHING MORE COMFORTABLE...
Leigh

© Leigh Rubin

© Leigh Rubin

© Leigh Rubin

© Leigh Rubin

When Neanderthals fall in love.

After Marcie leapt, Herb realized
it was just infatuation.

"Yes, Leroy, I'll forgive you for being unfaithful.
But I can never forget."

Simple solution for a happy relationship

As it was tamed, new ideas and attitudes transformed the Old West in different and unexpected ways.

"I appreciate your generous offer, Mr. Hefner, but I'm afraid we already have two bunnies on board."

...BUT WHAT IF I NEVER FIND MR. RIGHT?! I DON'T WANT TO END UP SPENDING THE REST OF MY LIFE ALONE!
Leigh

Effective birth-control methods of the South Pacific.

Max Planck—Brilliant physicist, lousy pick up artist

© Leigh Rubin

Emotional saddle baggage

© Leigh Rubin

Another fairy tale romance courtesy of the personal ads

Also ending in disaster was Custer's last one night stand.

"All day long, he smashes into other rams trying to impress me with his virility. But when *I'm* in the mood, *he* always has a headache!"

Leigh
HEY! WAIT A MINUTE! ACCORDING TO OUR PRENUPTIAL AGREEMENT YOU GET **EVERYTHING**... INCLUDING **ME**!
BURP.
WHY MALE BLACK WIDOWS SHOULD PAY CLOSE ATTENTION TO THE FINE PRINT.

"I just don't understand it. Why does Murray always get all the girls? What does he have that we don't?!"

"Oh sure, they may *seem* like the perfect couple, but rumor has it they have separate bank accounts."

© Leigh Rubin

The real and somewhat embarrassing cause of the mass extinction... reptile dysfunction.

© Leigh Rubin

"How come you never drag *me* around anymore?"

MY DRESS?! MY SHOES?! MY EARRINGS?! GOOD HEAVENS, HERB, JUST WHERE DO YOU THINK YOU'RE GOING?!
I GOT A JOB AT DAIRY QUEEN.
© Leigh Rubin

YOU SAY THAT YOU LOVE ME, BUT I WANT YOU TO RESPECT ME FOR MY BRAIN...WHAT LITTLE OF IT THERE IS.
© Leigh Rubin

Leigh
EVELYN, I WANT A DIVORCE.

© Leigh Rubin

"You realize, of course, that this could put a serious crimp in our plans for mating season."

© Leigh Rubin

"Why do scientists bother wasting their time on sheep?! If they cloned us it would certainly make *our* procreation process a lot less painful!"

© Leigh Rubin

"Of course I love you, Zelda. And nothing, with the sole exception of 150 degree asphalt, will ever come between us."

© Leigh Rubin

The sexual harassment suit that sent shock waves through the dairy industry.

SHE'S FROM VENUS!
HE'S FROM MARS!
FAMIL
COUN
SIGH... HERE WE GO AGAIN... SAME SOLAR SYSTEM, DIFFERENT WORLDS.
Leigh

...SO LET ME GET THIS STRAIGHT... YOUR BOYFRIEND IS JUST SITTING THERE MINDING HIS OWN BUSINESS WHEN YOU SNEAK UP BEHIND HIM AND PUSH?! ...BUT WHY?!
HUMPTY DUMPED ME!
Leigh

...AND IT'S MY PROFESSIONAL OPINION THAT THE PROBLEM WITH YOUR MARRIAGE IS AN OBVIOUS LACK OF COMMUNICATION.
leigh

"...Our nest egg, the place in the wetlands... My wife got *everything*... Talk about a loss of habitat."

"Hold on a minute there, loverboy... that's not *my* pollen on *your* collar!"

"Now I know it may seem impossible, but hopefully within a few sessions, we'll be able to clear the air between you two."

Just when bow ties came back in style, so did mating season.

HE'S SO UNPREDICTABLE!
I JUST DON'T UNDERSTAND HER BEHAVIOR!
FREQUENT COMPLAINTS HEARD BY SHARK MARRIAGE COUNSELORS
Leigh

"You knew I wasn't a vegetarian when we met. Did you honestly believe I would change just because we got married?"

"Listen, pal, for the last time... she's *mine*! So, keep your eyes off her!"

"Now there's a *real loser* for ya. Ernie can't even get lucky with an artificial flower!"

"Listen, Doc, as a species we've remained virtually the same for seventy million years... What makes her think she can change me *now*?!"

...WE'RE ALWAYS ON EDGE, CONSTANTLY BUTTING HEADS. LET'S FACE IT, LOUISE, OUR MARRIAGE IS ON THE ROCKIES.
Leigh

Moses pens his personal ad.

Evelyn's insecurity spoils the moment.

"No, Sidney, for the last time, I will *not* put that silly thing on and let you chase me around the house!"

Bernie, known as, "The King of One Night Stands," faces his greatest challenge.

© Leigh Rubin

© Leigh Rubin

UH OH! HERE COMES MY HUSBAND... YOU BETTER HIDE!
© Leigh Rubin

HOW TO TURN UP THE HEAT IN YOUR MARRIAGE
© Leigh Rubin

Another disappointing birthday in the redwoods.

"It's my wife... She's been hibernating...
with another bear."

A somewhat neglectful Davy receives his usual monthly reminder from the ex-Mrs. Crockett.

"For the last time, Hubert, sometimes 'Whoa!' really *does* mean 'Whoa!'"

Now that George had finally worked up the courage to slip an arm around Mary came the nagging question, "Which one?"

"OK, So I'm ill tempered!... Wouldn't you be if your wife ran around charging everything in sight?!"

MARRIAGE AND FAMILY COUNSELOR
THE PROBLEM IS THAT I ONLY WANT A LARGE FAMILY BUT SHE WANTS A **REALLY** LARGE FAMILY!
Leigh
© Leigh Rubin

"You're not going to believe this Sylvia, but I just saw Mildred pull up with a caterpillar! Why, she must be twice his age... talk about robbing the cocoon!"

The Black Widow support group

It was his first big trip to the city and Bernie was up for a good time.

The consequences of sexual harassment in the insect world

IT WAS LATER IN LIFE THAT EINSTEIN DISCOVERED THAT THERE WAS ONLY ONE THING CAPABLE OF TRAVELLING FASTER THAN THE SPEED OF LIGHT... GOSSIP.
Leigh

"Sid, Doris, I'd like you to meet Louise, my significant udder."

It was the little things that occasionally made Marcie suspicious.

"So you only gave the Easter Bunny a peck on the cheek? Well, then just how do you explain this?"

"I'm from the South, Louise, you're from the North. It could never work out between us... we're polar opposites."

WHY DON'T YOU EVER GIVE ME FLOWERS?

YOU SAY THAT YOU LOVE ME BUT HOW DO I KNOW YOU DON'T JUST WANT ME FOR MY BODY?
YOU DON'T HAVE ONE.
Leigh

I DON'T BELIEVE IT! MY WIFE AND MY BEST FRIEND! WELL, I'D LIKE TO SEE JUST HOW YOU TWO ARE GOING TO WIGGLE OUT OF THIS!
Leigh

TRUST ME, BUDDY, A FEW MORE SHOTS OF THIS STUFF AND SHE'LL TURN INTO A BEAUTIFUL SWAN.
Leigh

I DON'T SEE HOW WE CAN POSSIBLY HAVE ANY MEANINGFUL COMMUNICATION IN OUR RELATIONSHIP WHEN ALL HE EVER DOES IS **GRUNT**!
Leigh

© Leigh Rubin

"We may not have much, but at least we have each other, eh, babe?"

© Leigh Rubin

Popular cat pick up lines

Lois and Clark: The Golden Years

A seasoned crossing guard, Marie knew instinctively how to ward off unwanted advances.

Not even a sexy see-through nightie could revive Wanda's lifeless marriage.

"I'm tired of the singles scene... men leering at me as if I were a piece of meat."

"I don't know quite how to break this to you, Fellas, but I've found someone more fun."

Love at first sight strikes on the Kalahari.

"Seeing someone else?! Why, wherever would you get a silly idea like that?"

"What's the problem?! Didn't you tell me to pick up some milk on the way home?!"

"Stay away from my husband, you home wrecker!"

"Looks like from now on you'll be defending your own honor, Toots... Chivalry is dead."

Isaac Newton, brilliant physicist, mathematician, and pick up artist.

"My wife would kill me if she ever caught me spawning with anyone else. But since I'm gonna die anyway, it's kind of a 'win-win, lose-lose' no matter how you look at it."

Leigh
SET SAIL WITH ME ON A SEA OF LOVE
Romantic Genoese gentleman seeks first mate for the voyage of a lifetime. Come explore with me and together we can discover a whole new world of possibilities. If you're the one I'm searching for I'll travel to the ends of the Earth... figuratively speaking.
COLUMBUS' PERSONAL AD

He had always admired her from a distance, but never had the courage to break the ice.

Though very much in love, deep down, they knew it could never last. For in addition to their conflicting eating habits, it was a well-known fact that stripes and polka dots don't mix.

"I'm calling about your ad... It says you're looking for someone really spiritual?"

"Now I realize you both feel like ripping the stuffing out of each other, but perhaps I can help patch things up."

ESTHER AND HARRY TOOK A SHORT LIVED TRIP DOWN MEMORY LANE.
E+H

...AND THEN, AFTER ASCENDING TO THE THRONE, I SPENT THE NEXT FIFTY YEARS BUILDING COLOSSAL MONUMENTS TO MYSELF! BUT ENOUGH ABOUT **ME**...HOW'D YOU LIKE **MY** LAST PYRAMID?
(SIGH)... JUST WHAT I NEED... ANOTHER MAN THAT'S ALL WRAPPED UP IN HIMSELF!
Leigh

Turn every Bull into a Stud... Barnyard, the new fragrance from Cowvin Klein
Leigh

"It's positively nauseating. Ever since they met they've been practically inseparable."

"Don't be ridiculous. Of course I'm not afraid of intimacy... I just don't want to get close to you."

ME ?!...UNFAITHFUL?!
HOW COULD YOU SAY
SUCH A THING?!

"One girl on land and one in the pond... I'm telling ya, pal, being amphibious certainly has it's advantages."

"You've been a lot of fun, Wendell, but it's time for me to move on. Be strong, you'll survive without me... or not."

© Leigh Rubin

"At last, after five years at sea and a couple of thousand miles swimming upstream we're almost there. Yesiree, buddy, this is going to be our lucky night!"

© Leigh Rubin

"You realize, Louise, that in order for our symbiotic relationship to succeed there has to be at least some degree of trust."

Fairytale wedding... honeymoon disaster

"Isn't it romantic?... He whistled at her, she whistled back and right away they clicked!"

HEY, BABE, IF I TOLD YOU THAT YOU'VE REALLY GOT A PEEL WOULD YOU HOLD IT AGAINST ME?
Leigh
BANANA SMOOTHIE
© Leigh Rubin

Common adolescent affliction of the Antarctic: cold feet

It was destined to be another lonely night for Captain Ahab.

"So, c'mon, babe, what do you say?... Just you and me on a romantic migratory trip up the coast. It'd be perfectly safe... I've got international protection."

"Yessiree, the swinging 60's... Now *those* were the days. All that flower power and free love... I remember one time I pollinated an entire bouquet."

"Listen, buddy, for the last time, keep your paws off my wife or you'll end up with *two* blacker eyes!"

When Freudian slips reveal a less-than-perfect relationship.

THERE'S GOLDILOCKS... I'VE HEARD SHE'S SLEPT IN **EVERYONE'S** BED!
HOW VICIOUS RUMORS GET STARTED.

He was devastated. It was a John Deere letter. His tractor of twenty years had left him.

"Honestly, honey, I swear, it's nothing! She's just a decoy!"

Plato's frustrating love life.

Sylvia woke up next to some strange predator feeling cheap and humiliated. Once again, she had fallen for the old, "Let's live for the moment, tomorrow we could all be wiped out be a meteor," line.

JUST MARRIED
OZ 1
KANSAS

© Leigh Rubin

The early bird catches the worm... and then some.

© Leigh Rubin

"New muffler really keeps the car quiet, eh honey?"

The rough and often dangerous world of shark courtship.

Lydia awoke humiliated and alone. How could she have been so stupid? Hadn't her parents warned her never to get involved with free-range beef?

HOW MOTHS PREPARE FOR A BIG NIGHT OUT
EAU DE Pheramone
Leigh

"It's our love life doc. She never feels, well, you know... *frisky.*"

Smokey often enjoyed showing off his "trophy" wife.

"It's hard breaking up. ... Everywhere I turn I'm reminded of her."

"Can't you ever just forget about work and spend a romantic evening with me in front of the fire?!"

No matter how hard he tried, he couldn't shake the feeling that his wife had been unfaithful.

"Gee, fellas, I'd love to go out with you guys for a beer, but you know how it is once you tie the knot."

Leigh
DON'T BE RIDICULOUS...OF COURSE YOUR WIFE DOESN'T UNDERSTAND YOU. JUST BECAUSE WE'VE EVOLVED SPEECH DOESN'T MEAN WE'LL EVER SPEAK THE SAME LANGUAGE.

Perhaps Edna should have been more specific when placing her personal ad seeking "a big, strong, vegetarian, animal lover."

"It seems I underestimated their strength, Louise. Apparently wild horses *can* drag me away from you."

"Oh, darling, of course I want to marry you. But what would our families say? After all, I'm white and black and you're black and white."

"What's happened to us, Edna?... We used to be so *wild*."

Marcie made the foolish mistake of telling Herb that she needed her space.

When things don't quite turn out happily ever after.

Leigh
I DON'T KNOW WHY THIS IS COMING AS SUCH A SURPRISE TO YOU. WASN'T IT OBVIOUS ALL ALONG THAT WE'D INEVITABLY BREAK UP?

"Listen, doll, if it's a man you're after I think I have exactly what you're looking for in the way of husband material."

"Listen, honey, if you want to live in the land of make believe, be my guest. But if it's real life you're after, warts and all, you've got my number."

He was captivated by her beauty and wanted her desperately. But it was obvious she was spoken for.

"Are you crazy? What if my wife answered? I thought I told you...no mating calls at home!"

MOM, I'D LIKE YOU TO MEET MY NEW BOYFRIEND.
OH GREAT... I WONDER WHERE SHE DUG **HIM** UP!
Leigh

love is...
...blind
Leigh

JUNIOR'S BEEN ASKING ME WHERE LARVAE COME FROM AGAIN. I THINK IT'S ABOUT TIME YOU HAD A LITTLE CHAT WITH HIM ABOUT THE BIRDS AND US.
Leigh
© Leigh Rubin

About the Author

Leigh Rubin took his first steps on the path to cartoon success by creating a publishing company and distributing his own greeting cards. Rubes Publications, was established in 1979, and also published the popular Notable Quotes in 1981. Rubes®, in the form that cartoon aficionados now know it, began appearing in newspapers in 1984. The first paperback collection of Rubes® was published in late 1988 by G.P. Putnam & Sons. His most recent series of books include *The Wild Life of Cats, The Wild Life of Dogs, Pets,* Cows and *Farm Animals.* Originally self-syndicated, Rubes® is now distributed by Creators Syndicate, Inc. to more than 400 newspapers worldwide. As one of the most popular single-panel cartoons, Rubes® is a regular feature in SkyWest's *United Express* and *Delta Connections* magazines, and appears in such major daily metropolitan papers as the *San Diego Union Tribune*, the *Rochester Democrat and Chronicle*, the *Winnipeg Free Press*, the *Washington Times*, the *Houston Chronicle*, the *Orange County Register* and the *Los Angeles Daily News.*

Other books by Leigh Rubin

The Wild Life of Cats

The Wild Life of Dogs

The Wild Life of Pets

The Wild Life of Cows

The Wild Life of Farm Animals

Rubes® Bible Cartoons

Rubes® Then and Now

Calves Can Be So Cruel

Rubes®

Notable Quotes

Encore!

Amusing Arrangements

Sharks are People Too!